I0517892

THE LATEST NEWS FOR "MOTHER"

The
Universal Publishing
Association

That everyone who thirsteth for the truth may obtain it, this tract is mailed free of charge. It levies one exaction, the soul's obligation to itself to prove all things fast and hold fast that which is good. The only strings attached to this free proffer are the golden strands of Eden and the crimson cords of Calvary—the ties that bind.

Names and addresses of S.D.A.'s sent to us will be appreciated.

TRACT NO. 4

The Universal Publishing Association

P.O. Box 24027

Waco, Texas 76702

UniversalPublishing.com

ISBN: 978-1-962573-14-6

PRINTED IN U.S.A.

TOPICAL INDEX

JEZREEL'S INTRODUCTORY APPEAL

Dear "Ammi" and "Ruhamah":

   With deepest anxiety I am writing to implore you to make overtures to our estranged "Mother," that we may effect her reconciliation, save our Father from His inconsolable grief, and re-gladden our now unhappy home.

   I am in receipt of a letter from Father in which He reluctantly exposes our "Mother's" indecent worldly connection, and urges you to plead with her to repent of her unfaithfulness and to return to Him. He still calls for her with the same supreme love as always, though she has done a shameful thing, and is more corrupt in her inordinate love than are all women. So may your earnest prayer and diligent effort reunite our household and avert the imminent family disgrace, especially the shame and dishonor to Father's great name.

   If you truly love Father and "Mother," you will fervently respond to this solemn appeal. And what will be your gladness if by Father's merciful entreaties and your own untiring efforts, "Mother" be won to repentance, reconciled to Father, and restored to His kingly home! Think of the inexpressible joy, as with open arms He then receives the whole family and spreads a great banquet, as did the prodigal's father!

It is therefore my deepest concern that this urgent message reach you without delay. You will see that its warning is the most solemn and momentous since Noah's prediction of the flood.

In order to help in this crucial hour, it is necessary that we as true and loyal Seventh-day Adventists continue to be searchers of truth, wisdom, and knowledge of God. Make certain not to trip on the stumbling blocks of others, but to turn them into stepping stones to Christian progress.

The Jews before Christ's day, and ever since, thought they had all the truth there was to know. True, they had the Bible. But their consequent misunderstanding of the plan of God, and resultant over-confidence in themselves, led them to feel that they were rich and increased with goods and in need of nothing. It was this attitude that caused them to turn a deaf ear to the teachings of Christ the King of glory. Thus their misconception of the Truth, and their prejudice against light upon the Word of God, so robbed them of the knowledge and the wisdom of Jehovah that they were finally led, to their everlasting shame and condemnation, to commit the terrible crime of taking the life of the Son of God.

This fearful guilt, however, does not lie upon the hapless Jew alone. The Christian church as well, in each of her succeeding periods, has in effect crucified the

Saviour afresh in rejecting His messages of Present Truth to them. So it was in the days of Luther, of Knox, of Wesley, of Campbell, of Miller and of Sister White. And so it is today with all who are failing to take special heed to avoid the enemy's ever-set snare.

Now the only safe and sane procedure is to read closely every page of the solemn message contained herein. Let not a line escape your attention. Study every word carefully and prayerfully. Be an earnest and diligent student of the Truth. "Prove all things; hold fast that which is good." 1 Thess. 5:21.

As their record shows, the Bereans made a thorough and unbiased investigation of the messages which came to them, that they might know whether "those things" were so. In so doing they were neither misled by the enemy nor reproved by Inspiration, but rather were led by their open-mindedness to keep pace with the Truth, and were honored for their noble course. But the priests, whom God had previously made recipients of the Word, upon learning that the common people were hearing the Truth gladly, came and confused them. For this, those dignitaries were condemned—and all who gave heed to their voice rather than to the then unpopular one, were thus misled.

These things being written for our "en-samples," let us not fail to emulate the "more noble" example of the Bereans!

Only thus can we honestly exercise our judgment; otherwise we repeat the folly of the Jews who were led astray by the so-called wise teachers of Israel.

Says the Spirit of Prophecy: ". . . if a message comes that you do not understand, take pains that you may hear the reasons the messenger may give, comparing scripture with scripture, that you may know whether or not it is sustained by the Word of God. . . . No one of those who imagine that they know it all is too old or too intelligent to learn from the humblest of the messengers of the living God."—*Testimonies on Sabbath School Work*, pp. 65, 66; *Counsels on Sabbath School Work*, pp. 29, 30.

It is these so-called venial sins of becoming prejudiced and self-satisfied, and of leaning upon others, that have ever led God's people away from Him. Then, too, the fear of coming in contact with error has all too often kept them from coming in contact with advancing Truth. These pet fears and sins condoned by most Christians and even defended by many, have, at the introduction of each advancing Truth, robbed multitudes of eternal glory.

Ponder anew the experience of the people in the days of Paul: "And the brethren immediately sent away Paul and Silas by night unto Berea: who coming thither went into the synagogue of the Jews. These were more noble than those in Thessalonica, in that they received the Word with all readiness of mind, and searched the Scriptures daily, whether those things were so. Therefore many of them believed; also of honourable women which were Greeks, and of men, not a few. But when the Jews of Thessalonica had knowledge that the Word of God was preached of Paul at Berea, they came thither also, and stirred up the people." Acts 17:10-13.

Having thus briefly recalled to your minds the fatal mistake of the church throughout her long history, I now divulge the climaxing news: Father has promised to give forever to "Mother," Pisgah's View—His great vineyard—if she will return and be true! He will hedge it about with "a wall of fire" (Zech. 2:5), lay its "stones with fair colours," and its "foundations with sapphires," make its "windows of agates," and its "gates of carbuncles," and deck all its "borders of pleasant stones" (Isa. 54:11, 12), so that "there shall not come thither the fear of briers and thorns." Isa. 7:25.

I am confident that after hearing our Father's merciful plea in the succeeding pages, and then closely restudying this appeal, it will become the more urgent. Be assured that I shall rejoice to hear from all of you as to the results of your importuning "Mother."

Sincerely yours for a happy home,
JEZREEL
By V. T. H.

THE OLD AND NEW TESTAMENT CHURCH

HISTORY

DEPICTED BY ONE FAMILY

In the Old Testament obtained not mercy — but in the New shall obtain mercy - purifed

AMMI

RUHAMAH

JEZREEL

LOAMMI

LORUHAMAH

JEZREEL

B.C.

A.D.

HOSEA ONE AND TWO

"THE PEOPLE THAT DOTH NOT UNDERSTAND SHALL FALL." HOS. 4:14.

"THE DAYS ARE AT HAND, AND THE EFFECT OF EVERY VISION." EZEK. 12:23.

"AND SHALL FEAR THE LORD AND HIS GOODNESS IN THE LATTER DAYS." HOS. 3:5.

The Latest News for "Mother"
By Hosea
CHAPTERS ONE AND TWO

"The Word of the Lord that came unto Hosea, the son of Beeri, in the days of Uzziah, Jotham, Ahaz, and Hezekiah, kings of Judah, and in the days of Jeroboam the son of Joash, king of Israel. The beginning of the Word of the Lord by Hosea. And the Lord said to Hosea, Go, take unto thee a wife of whoredoms and children of whoredoms: for the land hath committed great whoredom, departing from the Lord.

"So he went and took Gomer the daughter of Diblaim; which conceived and bare him a son. And the Lord said unto him, Call his name Jezreel; for yet a little while, and I will avenge the blood of Jezreel upon the house of Jehu, and will cause to cease the kingdom of the house of Israel. And it shall come to pass at that day, that I will break the bow of Israel in the valley of Jezreel.

"And she conceived again, and bare a daughter. And God said unto him, Call her name Lo-ruhamah: for I will no more have mercy upon the house of Israel; but I will utterly take them away.

"But I will have mercy upon the house of Judah, and will save them by the Lord their God, and will not save them by bow, nor by sword, nor by battle, by horses, nor by horsemen.

"Now when she had weaned Lo-ruhamah, she conceived and bare a son. Then said God, Call his name Lo-ammi: for ye are not My people, and I will not be your God." Hos. 1:1-9.

From the foregoing scriptures, it is seen that Hosea's wife and children were such in vision only, and were therefore entirely figurative; they were so named as to make a fitting analogy of His people—Judah and Israel. And being of "whoredoms," they fittingly prefigure the idolatrous state of His church.

Continuing with the prophecy, we hear the Lord command Jezreel: "Say ye unto your brethren, Ammi; and to your sisters, Ruhamah." Hos. 2:1.

The same pair of children introduced in the first chapter of the vision are in the second chapter redenominated, the difference being that from both names is dropped the prefix "Lo" which, in the Hebrew, means "No." Accordingly, whereas Lo-ruhamah means "no mercy" and Lo-ammi "not My people", Ruhamah means "mercy" and Ammi "My people." Hos. 1:6; 2:4. See margin.

This change of status, implied in the change of names, denotes a division of church history. In one instance the membership is called "not My people," receiving "no mercy," and in the other instance "My people," receiving "mercy." The apostle Paul gave the key to this whole prophecy by revealing the interpretation of that part of it which met its fulfilment in his day:

"Even us, whom He hath called, not of the Jews only, but also of the Gentiles? As He saith also in Osee, I will call them My people, which were not My people;

and her beloved, which was not beloved. And it shall come to pass, that in the place where it was said unto them, Ye are not My people; there shall they be called the children of the living God." Rom. 9:24-26.

So we see that Chapter One of Hosea's vision foretells God's rejecting the Jews, which we know He did after they rejected His Son. At that time was fulfilled the sad pronouncement: "Ye are not My people, and I will not be your God." Yet in the very next breath, as it were, the Jews are called "the children of the living God." This paradox is cleared in Chapter Two, as it is in Romans 9: the Jews who did *not* reject Christ, but who became Christians, are the ones called "the children of the living God." Clearly, then, in the simultaneous fulfilment of these contrasting decrees were the death throes of the Jewish nation and the birth pangs of the Christian church.

Having now established that this scripture gives the termination of the one dispensation and the beginning of the other, we must next discover how far back in the history of the Old Testament division and how far forward in the history of the New Testament division, this prophetic allegory reaches:

"And I will give her her vineyards from thence, . . . and she shall sing there, as in the days of her youth, and as in the day when she came up out of the land of Egypt." Hos. 2:15.

When analyzed, this verse shows that the first division began in the days of Abraham, when the church was in "her youth"; continued on to her exodus from Egypt, the days when she "sang"; and terminated with the crucifixion of Christ, the hour that doomed Judaism.

The ensuing verses tell how far in the Christian division this personified prophecy reaches:

"And in that day will I make a covenant for them with the beasts of the field, and with the fowls of heaven, and with the creeping things of the ground: and I will break the bow and the sword and the battle out of the earth, and will make them to lie down safely.

"And I will betroth thee unto Me for ever; yea, I will betroth thee unto Me in righteousness, and in judgment, and in lovingkindness, and in mercies. I will even betroth thee unto Me in faithfulness: and thou shalt know the Lord. And it shall come to pass in that day, I will hear saith the Lord, I will hear the heavens, and they shall hear the earth." Hos. 2:18-21.

These verses describe the latter day state of the once fallen wife, the church, as one of unadulterated purity and absolute safety. But as she is at the present time still in her Laodicean condition, "wretched, and miserable, and poor, and blind, and naked," still impure and still in danger, it is evident that as Hosea's vision extends over the entire length of the Jewish church, it also extends over the entire length of the Christian church, from the crucifixion to her fast-approaching liberation from bondage, when the Lord is to hear the heavens, and the heavens are to hear the earth.

This one-family, dual symbolization of the Old and New Testament churches shows them to be one church. Accordingly, her character in both dispensations is dramatically personified—first, during

The Old Testament Period.

Some years after the tribes crossed the River Jordan and settled in the "promised land," their kingdom began to decline from its high spiritual estate. Finally, in the reign of Solomon, the Lord said to Jeroboam: "I will rend the kingdom out of the hand of Solomon, and will give ten tribes to thee: . . . because that they have forsaken Me." 1 Kings 11:31, 33.

This verdict was not executed until after the death of Solomon, when the ten tribes, upon revolting against Rehoboam, called Jeroboam and ". . . made him king over all Israel . . ." 1 Kings 12:20. But ". . . all the house of Judah, with the tribe of Benjamin . . ." (verse 21), remained to Rehoboam, son of Solomon. So it was that the kingdom was divided, the ten tribes, the kingdom of Israel, taking the northern portion of "the promised land," and the two tribes, the kingdom of Judah, retaining the southern portion.

But the decree, ". . . I will break the bow of *Israel* [the princes of the ten-tribe kingdom] in the valley of Jezreel" (Hos. 1:5), was not fulfilled until later when Jehu "slew all that remained of the house of Ahab in [the valley of] Jezreel, and all his great men, and his kinsfolks, and his priests, until he left him none remaining." 2 Kings 10:11.

"Thus Jehu destroyed Baal out of Israel, . . . but . . . took no heed to walk in the law of the Lord God of Israel with all his heart: . . . In those days the Lord began to cut Israel short: and Hazael smote them in all the coasts of Israel; . . . until the Lord removed Israel out of His sight, as He had said by all His servants the prophets. So was Israel carried away . . . to Assyria . . . and in the cities of the Medes." 2 Kings 10:28, 31, 32; 17:23; 18:11. Herewith came to pass the fore-warning: "I . . . will cause to cease the kingdom of the house of Israel." Hos. 1:4.

Not many years after the dispersion of the ten tribes, ". . . did Sennacherib king of Assyria come up against all the fenced cities of Judah, and took them . . . And the king of Assyria sent Tartan and Rabsaris, and Rabshakeh . . . with a great host against Jerusalem. . . ." 2 Kings 18:13, 17.

"And it came to pass, when king Hezekiah heard it, that he rent his clothes, and covered himself with sackcloth, and went into the house of the Lord . . . and . . . prayed before the Lord, and said, O Lord

God of Israel, which dwellest between the cherubim, Thou art the God, even Thou alone, of all the kingdoms of the earth; Thou hast made heaven and earth . . . Now therefore, O Lord our God, I beseech Thee, save Thou us out of his hand, that all the kingdoms of the earth may know that Thou art the Lord God, even Thou only.

"Then Isaiah the son of Amoz sent to Hezekiah, saying, Thus saith the Lord God of Israel, That which thou hast prayed to Me against Sennacherib king of Assyria I have heard. . . .

"And it came to pass that night, that the angel of the Lord went out, and smote in the camp of the Assyrians an hundred four-score and five thousand: and when they arose early in the morning, behold, they were all dead corpses." 2 Kings 19:1, 15, 19, 20, 35.

By this divine interposition, the Lord fulfilled His promise: "But I will have mercy upon the house of Judah, and will save them by the Lord their God, and will not save them by bow, nor by sword, nor by battle, by horses, nor by horsemen." Hos. 1:7.

Notwithstanding this great mercy, Judah continued to sin exceedingly against Him: "And the Lord God of their fathers sent to them by His messengers, rising up betimes, and sending; because He had compassion on His people, and on His dwelling place: but they mocked the messengers of God, and despised His words, and misused His prophets, until the wrath of the Lord arose against His people, till there was no remedy. Therefore He brought upon them the king of the Chaldees, who slew their young men with the sword in the house of their sanctuary, and had no compassion upon young man or maiden, old man, or him that stooped for age: He gave them all into his hand.

"And all the vessels of the house of God, great and small, and the treasures of the house of the Lord, and the treasures of the king, and of his princes; all these he brought to Babylon. And they burnt the house of God, and brake down the wall of Jerusalem, and burnt all the palaces thereof with fire, and destroyed all the goodly vessels thereof.

"And them that had escaped from the sword carried he away to Babylon; where they were servants to him and his sons until the reign of the kingdom of Persia." 2 Chron. 36:15-20.

After the appointed time of captivity, God remembered His promise of mercy to them, and ". . . stirred up the spirit of Cyrus king of Persia, that he made a proclamation throughout all his kingdom, and put it also in writing, saying, Thus saith Cyrus king of Persia, All the kingdoms of the earth hath the Lord God of Heaven given me; and He hath charged me to build Him an house in Jerusalem, which is in Judah." "And this house was finished on the third day of the month Adar, which was in the sixth year of the reign of Darius the king." 2 Chron. 36:22, 23; Ezra 6:15.

In so doing, God again kept His promises to Judah. But the ten tribes, Israel, He did not deliver, and thereby brought to pass His word: "I will no more have mercy upon the house of Israel." Hos. 1:6.

"Now when she had weaned Lo-ruhamah, she conceived, and bare a son. Then said God, Call his name Lo-ammi: for ye are not My people, and I will not be your God." Verses 8, 9.

In spite, though, of the Lord's repeated great mercy and wonderful deliverances in her behalf, Judah's continual sins finally led her utterly to forsake Him by denying His only begotten Son: "And they cried out all at once, saying, Away with this man, and release unto us Barabbas." Luke 23:18. Thus did Judah's backsliding at last bring upon her the dreadful anathema: ". . . ye are not My people, and I will not be your God." Hos. 1:9.

So far in this allegory, we see the history of the church up to the crucifixion of Christ. Now it is necessary to ascertain whether it contains the history of

The New Testament Period.

While, in Chapter One of his vision, Hosea describes the church's idolatrous

—19—

state in the Jewish dispensation, in Chapter Two he correspondingly describes the church's idolatrous state in the Christian dispensation.

"Say ye unto your brethren, Ammi; and to your sisters, Ruhamah. Plead with your mother, plead: for she is not My wife, neither am I her husband: let her therefore put away her whoredoms out of her sight, and her adulteries from between her breasts; lest I strip her naked, and set her as in the day that she was born, and make her as a wilderness, and set her like a dry land, and slay her with thirst.

"And I will not have mercy upon her children; for they be the children of whoredoms. For their mother hath played the harlot: she that conceived them hath done shamefully: for she said, I will go after my lovers, that give me my bread and my water, my wool and my flax, mine oil and my drink." Hos. 2:1-5.

In the Christian era the church started out in an even more advantageous spiritual condition than in the Jewish era. Besides, she could have profited by the example of the fallen Jews. But as the verses just quoted reveal, she utterly failed to do so. Instead, as with the passing of Joshua, the Jews began to depart from their God, so with the passing of the apostles, the Christians drifted likewise. In lowering the Christian standard and exalting the pagan, the church played the harlot with the heathen. In this way conceiving and bringing forth her so-called converts, "she . . . hath done shamefully," saith the Lord, "for she said, I will go after my lovers, that give me my bread and my water, my wool and my flax, mine oil and my drink."

These sentiments, she reflected by her attitude that her every candidate for membership, even those not fully converted to Christ, should nevertheless be baptized into the regular fellowship; meanwhile their financial support would further the work of God.

Reasoning like this is of a piece with that of the little girl who joyously exclaimed to her mother: "Look! I got a good bargain from the peddler! For this bagful of cherries, I was supposed to have given a pound of wool, but instead of giving all wool, I hid your gold bracelet in it!"

To give church membership to those who have not brought forth "fruit meet for repentance" is an even more costly stunt than to barter for cherries as though they were worth their weight in gold. Besides this foolish act of giving away shares in the church's estate, one cannot begin to count the cost of the demoralizing influence that such subversive "stockholders" exert upon the true people of God. By such folly, the early church unwittingly furthered the design of the Wicked Seed-sower, and also brought upon herself the Dark Ages of religion. Yet even in spite of this frightful consequence, which should have taught her unforgetably the lesson to consecrate her zeal to the building up of a Spirit-born membership only, she still continues heed-less in her

Zeal for Large Congregations.

A passion for increase of members without a com-mensurate burden for their sanctification—their be-ing "born again"—is engendered not by the Spirit of Christ, but rather by the carnal heart, which says: "I will go after my lovers, that give me my bread and my water, my wool and my flax, mine oil and my drink." Selfishness, ambition, greed—these are Satan's right-hand helpers.

Had the early Christian church continued in her first love for the salvation of souls and the advancement of the kingdom of Christ rather than for enlarging her membership, the enemy's operatives, the tares, could never have infiltrated into her ranks. But her zeal for purity waned, and she gave herself to the raising of goals—a selfish gain. "Yea," saith the prophet; "they are greedy dogs which can never have enough, and they are shepherds that cannot understand: they all look to their own way, every one for his gain, from his quarter." Isa. 56:11.

How fearful the lesson! Never is the prosperity of the church to be sought in silver and gold, and nev-er can she stand in the wisdom and power of men! Though money has its place in her economy, it is not her most urgent need. Upon fidelity to the message with which she has been entrusted, depends her only real success. This calls for men whom God can trust and upon whom He may freely pour His Spirit; men who will stand true to principle though the whole world turns against them; men who will in faith rise to the heights to which Christ bids: "Take no thought for your life, what ye shall eat, or what ye shall drink; nor yet for your body, what ye shall put on. . . . (For after all these things do the Gentiles seek:) for your heavenly Father knoweth that ye have need of all these things. But seek ye first the kingdom of God, and His righteousness, and all these things shall be added unto you. Take therefore no thought for the morrow: for the morrow shall take thought for the things of itself." Matt. 6:25, 32-34.

All who follow in the decadent trend of the Christian church, departing from the way of the Lord, and going in "a way which seemeth right unto a man" (Prov. 14:12), will experience

The Rod of God's Chastening.

"Behold, I will hedge up thy way with thorns, and make a wall, that she shall not find her paths. And she shall follow after her lovers, but she shall not overtake them; and she shall seek them, but shall not find them: then shall she say, I will go and return to my first husband; for then was it better with me than now. For she did not know that I gave her corn, and wine, and oil, and multiplied her silver and gold, which they prepared for Baal." Hos. 2:6-8.

When the church drifts with the current of the world, away from the Lord, He can no longer bless her, lest He drive her the faster downstream toward destruction. The only way that He can then save her and bring her back to Him, is to withdraw His helping hand from her until she finds herself grounded on a reef of her own folly, with the fierce waves of retribution beating over her sides. Then only will she respond to His voice.

God's method of bringing His church to a self-realization of her dangerous condition is portrayed in Christ's parable of the prodigal. Had the father denied the boy's request to go, the lad would forever have been embittered with a feeling of what he believed was his father's injustice, and no one could ever have convinced him that his father did not deprive him of the opportunity of winning great wealth and a name for himself. But his bitter experience along the husk-path of disillusionment taught him the great lesson in his life, as nothing else could ever have taught it to him.

This parable perfectly illustrates how wisely God deals with the church in her follies, and how her self-conceit and Laodicean wisdom prevent her profiting from the experience of others.

Instead of her overtaking (Christianizing) her lovers, they overtook (paganized) her. She "shall not find them," because she has failed to save them. Finally, after going through her prodigality, she will penitently return to her first Husband—the Lord. To hasten her return, the Lord overtakes her in the wilderness, thus fulfilling His word:

"Therefore will I return, and take away My corn in the time thereof, and My wine in the season thereof, and will recover My wool and My flax given to cover her nakedness. And now will I discover her lewdness in the sight of her lovers, and none shall deliver her out of Mine hand. I will also cause all her mirth to cease, her feast days, her new moons, and her sabbaths, and all her solemn feasts." Hos. 2:9-11.

Just as God chastened her in olden time by permitting Nebuchadnezzar, king of Babylon, to abolish the ceremonial system by destroying ancient Jerusalem and its temple, just so did He chasten her in the Christian era by permitting Rome to gain control over her and to supplant her true religious system by a counterfeit—a pagan priesthood and a pagan sabbath. Then was His word fulfilled: "I will also cause all her mirth to cease, her feast days, her new moons, and her sabbaths, and all her solemn feasts."

Since these ordinances (her feast days, her sabbaths, etc.) were part of "a compacted prophecy of the gospel, a presentation in which were bound up the promises of redemption" (*The Acts of the Apostles,* p. 14), and since Hosea's symbolization has brought us into the Christian era, the ceasing of the ordinances therefore typifies Rome's supplanting the Truth. Daniel, also, was shown that this was to be accomplished through Rome, the "exceeding great" horn, which "cast down . . . to the ground" the Truth "and the *place* of His [Christ's] sanctuary." Dan. 8:12, 11.

Note that the "Truth" and the "place," not the sanctuary itself were "cast down"; that is, both Christ's Truth and His *place* in the earthly sanctuary were set aside, so that the knowledge as to His mediatorial work became obscured. (For a detailed explanation of Daniel 8 and 9, see *The Shepherd's Rod*, Vol. 2, pp. 126-147; Tract No. 3, pp. 27-32.)

"And I will destroy," saith the Lord, "her vines and her fig trees, whereof she hath said, These are my rewards that my lovers have given me: and I will make them a forest, and the beasts of the field shall eat them. And I will visit upon her the days of Baalim, wherein she burned incense to them, and she decked herself with her earrings and her jewels [worldly display], and she went after her lovers [the world], and forgat Me, saith the Lord. Therefore, behold, I will allure her, and bring her into the wilderness [away from the vineyard—among the Gentiles], and speak comfortably unto her." Hos. 2:12-14.

This prediction was made over a thousand years before she lost her vineyards, and before she "fled into the *wilderness*, where she hath a place prepared of God, that they should feed her there a thousand two hundred and threescore days." Rev.

12:6. But while she was there in fugitive retreat from her own land, God spoke "comfortably unto her." In other words, she, like the wayward prodigal, had to have a bitter experience, longing again for home, before the Lord could do anything for her. Thus at the end of her exile, His overtures of love and mercy were to strike in her a truly responsive chord.

As we have already seen, this symbolism shows the Christian church endowed with the sanctuary truth (Hos. 2:11). And since the Seventh-day Adventist church is known to be the only one with this doctrine, it is evident that this symbolical prophecy of church history brings us this side of 1844 A. D. to the founding of the Seventh-day Adventist denomination. Consequently, the allegory now reveals her present condition, and God's counsel to her.

Moreover, the fact that the unfolding of these chapters is now for the first time brought to attention, further proves that the lessons which they contain are expressly for the church at this hour; the first of which to be considered is the lesson of

The Typical Valley of Achor.

"I will give her her vineyards from thence, and the valley of Achor for a door of hope." Hos. 2:15.

Whatever may be the meaning of the "valley of Achor," it is her "door of hope"

—the only way out of her predicament. To know why it is her door of hope, is naturally of most immediate interest.

Only three times in the Scriptures is "the valley of Achor" mentioned: once in a literal setting (Josh. 7:24, 26), and twice in a figurative setting (Isa. 65:10; Hos. 2:15). A study of the literal will give us the key that will unlock the meaning of the figurative.

The first city to fall into the hands of the Israelites upon their crossing the River Jordan, was Jericho. The command to Joshua was that the city, with every living thing in it, be destroyed, burned with fire, but that "all the silver, and gold, and vessels of brass and iron . . ." be "consecrated unto the Lord" and brought "into the treasury of the Lord." Josh. 6:19.

"But the children of Israel committed a trespass in the accursed thing," and as a result they began to fall before their enemies, whereupon "Joshua said, Alas, O Lord God, wherefore hast Thou at all brought this people over Jordan, to deliver us into the hand of the Amorites, to destroy us? would to God we had been content, and dwelt on the other side Jordan! O Lord, what shall I say, when Israel turneth their backs before their enemies! For the Canaanites and all the inhabitants of the land shall hear of it, and shall environ us round, and cut off our name from the earth: and what wilt Thou do unto Thy great name?

"And the Lord said unto Joshua, Get thee up; wherefore liest thou thus upon thy face? Israel hath sinned, and they have also transgressed My covenant which I commanded them: for they have even taken of the accursed thing, and have also stolen, and dissembled also, and they have put it even among their own stuff.

"Therefore the children of Israel could not stand before their enemies, but turned their backs before their enemies, because they were accursed: neither will I be with you any more, except ye destroy the accursed from among you. Up, sanctify the people, and say, Sanctify yourselves against tomorrow: for thus saith the Lord God of Israel There is an accursed thing in the midst of thee, O Israel: thou canst not stand before thine enemies, until ye take away the accursed thing from among you.

"In the morning therefore ye shall be brought according to your tribes: and it shall be, that the tribe which the Lord taketh shall come according to the families thereof; and the family which the Lord shall take shall come by households; and the household which the Lord shall take shall come man by man." Josh. 7:1, 7-14.

"And Achan . . . was taken." And he "answered Joshua, and said, Indeed I have sinned against the Lord God of Israel, and thus and thus have I done: when I saw among the spoils a goodly Babylonish garment, and two hundred shekels of silver, and a wedge of gold of fifty shekels weight, then I coveted them, and took them; and, behold, they are hid in the earth in the midst of my tent, and the silver under it.

"And Joshua, and all Israel with him, took Achan the son of Zerah, and the silver, and the garment, and the wedge of gold, and his sons, and his daughters, and his oxen, and his asses, and his sheep, and his tent, and all that he had: and they brought them unto the *Valley of Achor*.

"And Joshua said, Why hast thou troubled us? The Lord shall trouble thee this day. And all Israel stoned him with stones, and burned them with fire, after they had stoned them with stones." Verses 18, 20, 21, 24, 25.

At that solemn time, Achan was the only sinner in the camp, but because of his sin the whole nation was about to fall and thus God's great name be dishonored in the eyes of the heathen.

The Lord's dealings with Joshua reveal that *His servants* must vigilantly watch that no evil enter into their ranks, and that His words through His prophets be feared as though He Himself were speaking directly to the people.

When Joshua proclaimed that "there is an accursed thing in the midst of thee, O

Israel" (Josh. 7:13), Achan concealed his guilt as long as possible instead of immediately confessing it. When finally it was brought to light and he was taken, he "answered Joshua, and said, Indeed I have sinned against the Lord God of Israel." But, alas, it was too late then for God either to accept his confession and pardon his sin or to vindicate His people unless they fulfilled their obligation to deal with the sinner strictly in accordance with the manner He had prescribed.

"Now all these things happened unto them for ensamples: and they are written for our admonition, upon whom the ends of the world are come. Wherefore let him that thinketh he standeth take heed lest he fall." 1 Cor. 10:11, 12.

The valley of Achor of Joshua six and seven, therefore, is a type of the valley of Achor of Hosea two.

With the key here in hand, we are now to unlock the mystery connected with "the door of hope," and discover what Present Truth lesson lies within

The Antitypical Valley of Achor.

Had not this remarkable judicial writ been intended for "an ensample," God would not have designated the very place of Achan's punishment. His execution, then, in the valley of Achor, points forward to the time of an antitypical execution within the Christian church. Hence, this antitypical valley of Achor, her door of hope, can but point to the destruction of the sinners, tares in her midst, her illegitimate children. (See *Testimonies*, Vol. 5, p. 80.)

Unmistakably, the type shows that during this purification, God will destroy not only every sinner among His people but also their families and all their belongings with them. "The sieve is moving," declares the Spirit of Truth. "Let us not say, Stay Thy hand, O God. The church must be purged, and it will be." "And I saw that the Lord was whetting His sword in Heaven to cut them down. Oh that every lukewarm professor could realize the *clean work* that God is about to make among His professed people!"—*Testimonies,* Vol. 1, pp. 100, 190.

The type also shows that God will undertake this "clean work . . . among His professed people," just before He entrusts them with His very last message to the world—the message of "the great and dreadful day of the Lord" (Mal. 4:5). The power of this dreadful day is to lighten the earth with its glory (Rev. 18:1), and enable His people to re-possess the anti-typical promised land—the earth. So when the worthless material is consumed, the church, "clad in complete armor of light and righteousness, . . . enters upon her final conflict . . . and the influence of the truth testifies to the

world of its sanctifying, ennobling character. . . ."—
Testimonies to Ministers, pp. 17, 18.

Thus "this gospel of the kingdom shall be preached in all the world for a witness unto all nations; and then shall the end come." Matt. 24:14.

All these—the imminent purification of the church, the ensuing Loud Cry of the Third Angel's Message, and the restoration of the kingdom in the land of our fathers, with the subsequent conquering of the nations,—all these the type demands; demands them because Achan was executed and the camp freed from sinners before ancient Israel could conquer the "promised land."

Accordingly, after her purification, after she has taken heed to the call of Isaiah 52:1, then "clad in the armor of Christ's righteousness, the church is to enter upon her final conflict. 'Fair as the moon, clear as the sun, and terrible as an army with banners,' she is to go forth into all the world, conquering and to conquer."—*Prophets and Kings*, p. 725.

The prophet Ezekiel, also, was given a vision of this final purification of the church. His prophecy reveals that everyone who fails to receive the mark, or seal, is to fall under the slaughter of the "five men," and that all, "old and young, both maids, and little children, and women" will "all perish together" (*Testimonies*,

Vol. 5, p. 211; Ezek. 9:6), as typified by Achan's destruction—the "ensample."

This unassailable sequence of facts only bulwarks the Spirit of Prophecy's position that "this sealing of the servants of God is the same that was shown to Ezekiel in vision"; that "the true people of God . . . will always be on the side of faithful and plain dealing with sins which easily beset the people of God. Especially in the *closing work for the church*, in the *sealing time* of the one hundred and forty-four thousand . . . "—*Testimonies to Ministers*, p. 445; *Testimonies*, Vol. 3, p. 266.

Observe how definitely the foregoing testimony places the purification of the church before the gospel work is finished, and immediately before the Loud Cry of the Third Angel's Message is sounded. It clearly states that "the closing work for the church" is "the sealing time of the one hundred and forty-four thousand." And the fact that these are the "firstfruits," proves that this work for the church is the commencement of the "harvest," and that after they are sealed and the church purified, a second fruits are to be gathered in, for where there is no second gathering, there can be no "first."

This twofold harvest is brought to view also in Revelation 7. After beholding the gathering, the sealing of the one hundred and forty-four thousand firstfruits, John saw the subsequent ingathering of the "great multitude" out of all nations (verse 9)—the second fruits.

Developing still further the subject of the purification, the Spirit of Prophecy discloses that "those who have proved themselves unfaithful will not then be entrusted with the flock." But "the Lord has faithful servants who in the shaking, testing time will be *disclosed to view*." In other words, after the old set of servants, who have unfitted themselves for service, are put away, and the church thereby purified, God will then "disclose to view" the faithful and true, those whom He can trust as under-shepherds of His flock.

In this same connection, the Spirit of Prophecy also warns that "the days of purification of the church are hastening on apace. God will have a people pure and true. In the mighty sifting soon to take place, we shall be better able to measure the strength of Israel. The signs reveal that the time is near when the Lord will manifest that His fan is in His hand, and He will thoroughly purge His floor . . . Those who have trusted to intellect, genius, or talent, will not then stand at the head of rank and file. They did not keep pace with the light. Those who have proved themselves unfaithful will not then be entrusted with the flock. In the last solemn work few great men will be engaged. They are self-sufficient, independent of God, and He cannot use them. The Lord has faithful servants, who in the shaking, testing time will be disclosed to view."—*Testimonies*, Vol. 5, p. 80.

The words "thoroughly purge His floor" denote an absolute purging which leaves her without spot, wrinkle, or any such thing. Not until this "clean work" is accomplished, can God logically say to those who are in Babylon: "Come out of her, My people, that ye be not partakers of her sins, and that ye receive not of her plagues." Rev. 18:4. Indeed, were He to do no better than simply bring them into another place where sin still abounds, He might far better leave them right where they are. This final work for the church, being of such great importance, is still further elucidated in the prophecy of Malachi 3.

Of this impending purge, hope-inspiring and heartening to the righteous, but terrifyingly sorrowful to the wicked, the prophet declares: He "shall suddenly come to His temple [the church or "floor"], . . . but who may abide the day of His coming? and who shall stand when He appeareth? for He is like a refiner's fire, and like fullers' sope: and He shall sit as a refiner and purifier of silver: and He shall purify the sons of Levi, and purge them as gold and silver, that they may offer unto the Lord an offering in righteousness." Mal. 3:1-3.

In explanation of this scripture, the denomination-al publication (published and owned by the denomination as well as endorsed and used by the Sabbath School Department throughout the world in 1929), *Isaiah, the Gospel Prophet,* Vol. 3, p. 49, says: "Verse 20. [Isa. 59.] 'The Redeemer shall come to Zion.' This is *not* the coming *in the clouds,* but coming to the *church.* And when He comes, He will do the work mentioned in Malachi 3:1-3."

This official exposition of the text shows that in 1929 the denomination taught that the prophecy of Malachi 3, promising a thorough work of purification, is a message to the church.

Proceeding from Malachi's disclosure of the purification of the sons of Levi, the lesson leads us to the law of

The First-born, The First Fruits.

In God's original plan, the first-born of every family were to be the ministers of the temple. The "first-born" of the flesh, therefore, are the type of the first-born of the Spirit.

And though the typical first-born lost their priestly inheritance to the Levites, yet in the restitution of all things, in the final Davidian Period (Acts 15:16), this office will be restored to the antitypical first-born, the firstfruits of the harvest (Rev. 14:4), for they are "the servants of our God." Rev. 7:3. This restoration, therefore, is to follow their

Absolute Reformation, Resulting in Perfect Safety.

If with but *one* Achan in the camp, the Israel of Joshua's time was powerless to stand before the heathen, then what hope has modem Israel, with *hundreds* of Achans (*Testimonies*, Vol. 5, p. 157) in *her* midst, to stand through the approaching "time of trouble, such as never was since there was a nation"? Today as yesterday, there is for her but one "door of hope"—"the valley of Achor." There setting her free from sinners forever, God will then bring her out jubilantly singing as in the days of her "youth" and as in the day when she came up "out of the land of Egypt."

"And it shall be at that day, saith the Lord, that thou shalt call me Ishi; and shalt call Me no more Baali." Hos. 2:16.

She shall then no longer call Him "my Lord," but rather "my Husband" (margin). The relationship of a husband being closer than that of a lord, it denotes an elevation to a more intimate connection and walk with God. And that this elevation is the direct result of reformation, is evidenced in the words:

"For I will take away the names of Baalim out of her mouth, and they shall no more be remembered by their name." Verse 17.

This is because they have their ". . . Father's name written in their foreheads

. . . And in their mouth was found no guile: for they are without fault before the throne of God." Rev. 14:1, 5.

When God has taken His people through this "refining, purifying process" (*Testimonies*, Vol. 3, p. 541), and has brought them forth as fine gold seven times purified, with the dross burned out forever, then will He be able to fulfil His promise:

"And in that day will I make a covenant for them with the beasts of the field, and with the fowls of heaven, and with the creeping things of the ground: and I will break the bow and the sword and the battle out of the earth, and will make them to lie down safely." Hos. 2:18.

In spite of the ultimate joy and glory unsurpassed which this message of hope sets before the angel of the Laodiceans, who is in charge of the candlestick, the church, he is still

Warring Against the Message.

If God's people but sufficiently sensed their unpreparedness to meet the coming crisis, and could but see themselves standing, as it were, before the mouth of the dragon, they would tremble and faint for fear. But, alas, the pall of insensibility enveloping them is so great that he who comes as a harbinger of hope and release, instead of being gratefully welcomed, is viciously attacked as though he were a fiendish Harpy or some Gorgon- or Hydra-headed monster; and all because they know not the hour of their visitation, when the Lord will destroy them in His fury, and save the righteous in

His Mercy.

The fact that the names of the children in Hosea's vision are Lo-ruhamah (no mercy) and Lo-ammi (not My people) when representing the Old Testament period, signifies, as previously seen, that God could no longer extend mercy to the members of His church. So when He punished them by the heathen, the innocent suffered alike with the guilty. But the names Ruhamah (mercy) and Ammi (My people) show that now, in the latter day period, He will have mercy upon them by destroying the wicked only, sparing all the righteous.

"Behold, the days come, saith the Lord, that I will sow the house of Israel and the house of Judah with the seed of man, and with the seed of beast. And it shall come to pass, that like as I have watched over them, to pluck up, and to break down, and to throw down, and to destroy, and to afflict; so will I watch over them, to build, and to plant, saith the Lord. In those days they shall say no more, The fathers have eaten a sour grape, and the children's teeth are set on edge. But every one shall die for his own iniquity: every man that eateth the sour grape, his teeth shall be set on edge." Jer. 31:27-30.

Plainly, therefore, the constituency of the church in both periods is depicted by the same two children, Lo-ruhamah and Lo-ammi, except that in the latter period their names are altered.

The Scripture, "she shall sing there [in the New Testament period], as in the days of her youth [as in her first state in the Old Testament period], and as in the day when she came up out of the land of Egypt" (Hos. 2:15), attests that the experience of God's ancient people in going out of Haran, and out of Egypt, will be repeated at the present time: "And there shall be an highway for the remnant of His people, which shall be left, from Assyria; like as it was to Israel in the day that he came up out of the land of Egypt." Isa. 11:16. Thus "in that day shall the Branch of the Lord be beautiful and glorious, and the *fruit* of the earth shall be *excellent* and comely for them that are escaped of Israel.

"And it shall come to pass, that he that is left in Zion, and he that remaineth in Jerusalem, shall be called holy, even *every one* that is written *among the living* in Jerusalem: *when* the Lord shall have *washed away* the filth of the daughters of Zion, and shall have purged the blood of Jerusalem from the midst thereof by the spirit of judgment, and by the spirit of burning."

"And the Lord will create upon *every* dwelling place of mount Zion, and upon her assemblies, a *cloud* and smoke by day, and the shining of a *flaming fire* by night: for upon all the glory shall be a defence. And there shall be a tabernacle for a shadow in the daytime from the heat, and for a place of refuge, and for a covert from storm and from rain." Isa. 4:2-6.

This glorified repetition of God's leading an exodus movement by the shepherd's rod, shows that He is again using the same method to bring modern Israel out of the nations. Where the Jews failed to make their kingdom a working model of Theocracy, ordained solely to manifest God's power and thus convert the world to their precious Faith, the present kingdom movement must succeed. God's plans know no final failure; sooner or later, they will be carried out. (See *Patriarchs and Prophets*, p. 283.)

So today, in the antitype, "the Lord's voice crieth unto the city [church], and the man of wisdom [the teachable] shall see thy name: hear ye the rod, and Who hath appointed it." Mic. 6:9. "And by a prophet the Lord brought Israel out of Egypt, and by a prophet was he preserved." Hos. 12:13.

Obviously, therefore, God will pity all who come under the authority of His Rod today, confessing their sins and seeking mercy. But He will have no mercy upon the disobedient, not even upon any who covet

The Babylonish Garment of Today.

By Achan's illicit possession of the "goodly Bab-ylonish garment" is typified that class of church members who covet the worldly styles and fashions in vogue now, when Israel of today is about to enter the promised land. And the price he paid, they shall pay. (Read Isa. 3:16-26.) And not only they shall pay it, but also those who, following in the next steps of Achan,

Covet Silver and Gold.

Achan's taking the Lord's money represents that class of church members who covet the "silver" and the "gold" which He has set apart for Himself, and who thereby rob Him of that which is His Own—tithes and offerings. Those who withhold that which is His, and appropriate it for use according to their own wisdom, as well as those who oppress "the hire-ling in his wages, the widow, and the fatherless, and that turn aside the stranger from his right, and fear not Me, saith the Lord of hosts" (Mal. 3:5), are acting Achan's part, and therefore, "are cursed with a curse: . . . even this whole nation." Mal. 3:9.

The tithes and the offerings are of the Lord's sub-stance, and those who think that they can so manip-ulate them as to accomplish whatever end is desired, are deceiving themselves, not God, for His command is, "*Bring ye all* the tithes *into the store-*

house, that there may be meat in *Mine* house." Mal. 3:10. The storehouse is the only place designated where one may bring the tithes and offerings and unload from his shoulders the heavy responsibility which a faithful stewardship imposes. To do otherwise with them, is to leave one's account in the heavenly ledger standing in the red, even though one may appropriate them to some meritorious work of charity. While it is yet today, therefore, flee from this sin of Achan before it is forever too late! "As I live, saith the Lord God, I have no pleasure in the death of the wicked; but that the wicked turn from his way and live: turn ye, turn ye from your evil ways; for why will ye die, O house of Israel?" Ezek. 33:11.

Those who will today hear His voice and harden not their hearts as in the day of provocation, will He make

His Future Servants.

"Not by might, nor by power, but by My Spirit, saith the Lord of hosts." Zech. 4:6. In other words, the workers will be "taught rather by the unction of His Spirit, than by the outward training of scientific institutions. . . . God will manifest that He is not dependent on learned, self-important mortals." "The most weak and hesitating in the church, will be as David—willing to do and dare."—*Testimonies*, Vol. 5, pp. 82, 81.

Moreover, "I will take illiterate men, obscure men," says the Lord, "and move upon them by My Spirit, to carry out My purposes in the work of saving souls. The last message of mercy will be given by a people who love and fear Me."—*Review and Herald*, Sept. 21, 1905. "He will use men for the accomplishment of His purpose whom some of the brethren would reject as unfit to engage in the work."—*Review and Herald*, Feb. 9, 1895.

To these workers the Lord is graciously saying: "And strangers shall stand and feed your flocks, and the sons of the alien [those who are not of the 144,000] shall be your plowmen and your vinedressers. But ye shall be named the Priests of the Lord: men shall call you the Ministers of our God: ye shall eat the riches of the Gentiles, and in their glory shall ye boast yourselves." Isa. 61:5, 6. What an exalted privilege to be able to acknowledge no master but Christ, and to engage only in His work and live on His substance!

As this ministry, of which "there hath not been ever the like, neither shall be any more after it, even to the years of many generations" (Joel 2:2), is to be free from all earthly encumbrances, therefore let no one longer delay in effecting the transition which will ultimately see him engaged heart and soul in the Lord's "closing work for the church," the ingathering of the "firstfruits" who are to be sealed from among the living. And while giving himself to this work, he will at the same time be preparing himself to give the message in the time of the "Loud Cry," which the purification of the church—the deliverance of the sealed and the destruction of the unsealed—is to usher in, and which those who are to be purified are to proclaim.

Let each one wisely make this imperative transition by gradually curtailing pursuit of his own interests, and increasing pursuit of the Lord's. In this way, each one will steadily climb from an empty and unsung past of self-enterprise, to a full and glorious future of divine enterprise which shall call forth "from the uttermost part of the earth . . . songs, even glory to the righteous." Isa. 24:16.

"Let me tell you," says the Spirit of Prophecy, "if your heart is in the work, and you have faith in God, you need not depend upon the sanction of any minister or any people: if you go right to work in the name of the Lord, in a humble way doing what you can to teach the truth, God will vindicate you. If the work had not been so restricted by an impediment here and an impediment there, and on the other side an impediment, it would have gone forward in its majesty. It would have gone in weakness at first; but the God of heaven lives."—*Review and Herald*, April 16, 1901. (See also *Testimonies*, Vol.7, p. 25.)

My brethren, if you choose to have a part in this grandest-of-all work, the crowning act in the redemption of the world, you must now quickly make ready. Let not the cares of this life rob you of the crown of eternal life. Do not offer excuses for not making the change; stand not on the side of those who shall say: "I have bought a piece of ground, and I must needs go and see it: I pray thee have me excused"; or, "I have bought five yoke of oxen, and I go to prove them: I pray thee have me excused"; or, "I have married a wife, and therefore I cannot come." Luke 14:18-20. "For all that is in the world, the lust of the flesh and the lust of the eyes, and the pride of life, is not of the Father, but is of the world. And the world passeth away, and the lust thereof: but he that doeth the will of God abideth for ever." 1 John 2:16, 17.

Therefore, while yet engaged in your present occupation, go ye into the vineyard of the Lord, and as your interest there grows, let your private interests be diminishing until you find yourselves completely divorced from them and wedded to the Lord's.

"Time," says the Spirit of Prophecy, "is short, and our forces must be organized to do a larger work. Laborers are needed who comprehend the greatness of the work, and who will engage in it, not for the wages they receive, but from a realization of the nearness of the end. The time demands greater efficiency and deeper consecration. O, I am so full of this subject that I cry to God, 'Raise up and send forth messengers filled with a sense of their responsibility, messengers in whose hearts self-idolatry, which lies at the foundation of all sin, has been crucified.'"—*Testimonies*, Vol. 9, p. 27.

But as the harvest is great, and the laborers few, heaven is compelled to "finish the work, and cut it short in righteousness" (Rom. 9:28). Hence, the Lord Himself now will

Take Charge of the Flock.

"And I will betroth thee unto Me forever," saith the Lord, "yea, I will betroth thee unto Me in righteousness, and in judgment, and in lovingkindness, and in mercies. I will even betroth thee unto Me in faithfulness: and thou shalt know the Lord." Hos. 2:19, 20.

"They that trust in the Lord shall be as mount Zion, which cannot be removed, but abideth for ever. As the mountains are round about Jerusalem, so the Lord is round about His people from *henceforth* even for ever." Ps. 125:1, 2.

"And it shall come to pass in that day, I will hear, saith the Lord, I will hear the heavens, and they shall hear the earth." Hos. 2:21.

While the phrase, "I will hear the heavens," shows that He is on the earth, the phrase, "they shall hear the earth," shows that "by means of the angels there will be constant communication between heaven and earth."—*Testimonies*, Vol. 9, p. 16.

He "will use ways and means by which it will be seen that He is taking the reins in His own hands. The workers will be surprised by the simple means that He will use to bring about and perfect His work of righteousness."—*Testimonies to Ministers*, p. 300. And so God will "take charge of the flock Himself."—*Testimonies*, Vol. 5, p. 80. (See also our Tract No. 1.)

Having taken charge of the first-born, the first fruits of the harvest, He will use them to gather

The Second Fruits.

"And the earth shall hear the corn, and the wine, and the oil; and they shall hear Jezreel." Hos. 2:22.

The first clause makes clear that when the Lord Himself takes complete charge of the flock, a great harvest of souls is to be garnered in, for the earth shall hear the corn and the wine, and the oil—the spiritual food, the message. And they [his brethren in the church and in the world] shall hear "Jezreel"—the messengers.

"And I will sow her unto Me in the earth; and I will have mercy upon her that had not obtained mercy; and I will say to them which were not My people, Thou art My people; and they shall say, Thou art my God." Hos. 2:23.

The promise, "I will sow [multiply] her unto me *in the earth*," bears further substantiation that there is to be an ingathering of souls after the purification. Hence Jezreel's message accomplishes all this before the final close of probation—that for the world.

This evidence upon evidence makes clear that after the 144,000 are sealed and separated from among the wicked in the church, God "will send . . . them unto the nations," where "they shall *declare*" His "glory among the *Gentiles*. And they shall bring *all* your brethren for an offering unto the Lord out of *all* nations . . . in a clean vessel into the house of the Lord." Isa. 66:19, 20.

Hosea's family-allegory further shows that in the time of Jezreel's message, the whole world shall behold the glorified relationship of

The Father, Mother, and Children.

Hosea's wife being representative of the Lord's wife (Hos. 2:2), Hosea himself is a representative of the Lord. And since His wife is His church, she and her children are a representation of His church-family— ministers and laity. She represents the ministers because they bring forth the converts, the children that make up the laity. To Jezreel, Hosea's first-born son in the vision, comes the command:

"Say ye unto your brethren, Ammi; and to your sisters, Ruhamah. Plead with your mother, plead: for she is not My wife, neither am I her husband: let her therefore put away her whoredoms out of her sight, and her adulteries from between her breasts." Hos. 2:1, 2.

From this we see that Jezreel, the one addressed, is symbolical of a prophet who is to command his "brethren, Ammi," and his "sisters, Ruhamah," to go to their "mother" and plead with her to reform. The names, Ruhamah and Ammi, represent a brother and a sister (singular), but in commissioning Jezreel to speak to them, the Lord designates them in the plural,—"brethren" and "sisters," embracing the entire church membership.

Obviously, therefore, God ordained that one of the laity, Jezreel, His chosen agent, was to herald the message to Ammi and Ruhamah, his "brethren" and "sisters," who in turn were to plead with their "mother," the ministry. The Lord has plainly made known this procedure because He knew that the majority are ever prone to lean on their ministers for revelation of truth and because they forget the tragic fact that "in the closing work" for the church in each period, the ministry kept the flock from accepting advancing Truth, rather than leading them into It.

Truly "it is not enough to have good intentions; . . . not enough to do what a man thinks is right, or what the minister tells him is right. His soul's salvation is at stake, and he should search the Scriptures for himself. However strong may be his convictions, however confident he may be that the minister knows what is truth, this is not his foundation."

"The most humble and devoted in the churches were usually the first to receive the message."

"This truth has been repeatedly illustrated in the history of the church. . . . many of the professed followers of Christ refused to receive the light from heaven, and, like the Jews of old, knew not the time of their visitation. Because of their pride and unbelief, the Lord passed them by, and revealed His truth to those who, like the shepherds of Bethlehem and the Eastern magi, had given heed to all the light they had received."—*The Great Controversy*, pp. 598, 372, 316.

With the abundance of evidence herein made available to all, no one need remain in ignorance of the source through which the Lord reveals Himself, if each will but

Investigate Personally.

Graphically has the Lord again made known that it is perilous to make "flesh your arm"—to entrust to someone the personal responsibility of investigating "a message that comes in the name of the Lord." Each must for himself prove "all things" and hold fast to "that which is good," as every true child of God has ever done. Those who will not take time and pains to do this, are not honest with themselves or with God, and their interest in the kingdom of heaven is not such as that shown in the parable of the merchant man who sought salvation as though seeking for "goodly pearls" or "hidden treasure." Matt. 13:44, 45. And those who cannot for themselves discern the difference between truth and error, are prefigured by the "five *foolish* virgins." Matt. 25:2.

But there is still another class who, from pride of opinion and for fear that in coming to the light they may have their errors exposed to view, refuse to discharge their individual responsibility, and consequently remain in the darkness. Still others hold back from openly taking their stand by the side of those who advocate plain but unpopular truth, because of the inconvenience, reproach, and persecution which follow in the wake of being cast out of the synagogue.

So the sins of prejudice, pride, and cowardice work like a cancer in the heart, lurking beneath the surface, only to rob their host of eternal glory.

". . . they are drunken, but not with wine; they stagger, but not with strong drink. For the Lord hath poured out upon you the spirit of deep sleep, and hath closed your eyes: *the prophets and your rulers, the seers hath He covered.* And the vision of all [the prophets] is become unto you as the words of a book that is sealed, which men deliver to one that is learned, saying, Read this, I pray thee: and he saith, I cannot; for it is sealed [not essential to salvation, etc.]: and the book is delivered to him that is not learned, saying, Read this, I pray thee: and he saith, I am not learned [I must see so and so about it].

"Wherefore the Lord said, Forasmuch as this people draw near Me with their mouth, and with their lips do honour Me, but have removed their heart far from Me, and their fear toward Me is taught by the precept of men: therefore, behold, I will proceed to do a marvelous work among this people, even a marvelous work and a wonder: for the wisdom of their wise men shall perish, and the understanding of their prudent men shall be hid." Isa. 29:9-14.

From this bill of indictment which God has drawn up against those who profess to be His, we see that their ignorance is the result of their

Rejection of the Prophets.

Every succeeding Jewish generation rejected the living prophets, at the same time bearing recognition and honor to the preceding ones who were slain by, and for speaking to, the fathers. Thus Jesus rebuked them, saying: "Woe unto you, scribes and Pharisees, hypocrites! because ye build the tombs of the prophets, and garnish the sepulchres of the righteous, and say, If we had been in the days of our fathers, we would not have been partakers with them in the blood of the prophets." Matt. 23:29, 30.

Most of the Christians at the present time, by despising the gift of prophecy in the Christian era, and by applying the Old Testament Scriptures to God's ancient people only, have rejected all the prophets! The Seventh-day Adventist denomination, however, has long professed to believe in the Spirit of Prophecy, particularly in that special message which in the latter part of the last century make clear that the angel of Revelation 18:1, who is to lighten the earth with his glory, was still in the future (*Early Writings*, p. 277), and that the prophet Elijah's message was yet to come (*Testimonies to Ministers*, p. 475). In her Laodicean attitude, however, that she is "rich, and increased with goods," and has "need of nothing," neither truth nor prophets, she manifests the spirit which led the Jewish leaders to kill God's messengers, and which has caused nearly all Christendom to set aside the prophets, thus teaching that they ceased with the preach-ing of John the Baptist.

By thus shortening man's vision, the enemy is determinedly preparing the way for the church to reject the latter rain, and never to receive the promised latter-day Pentecost:

"Be glad then, ye children of Zion, and rejoice in the Lord your God: for He hath given you the former rain moderately, and He will cause to come down for you the rain, the former rain, and the latter rain in the first month. . . . And it shall come to pass *afterward*, that I will pour out My Spirit upon all flesh; and your sons and your daughters shall *prophesy*, your old men shall dream dreams, your young men shall see visions: and also upon the servants and upon the handmaids in those days will I pour out My Spirit." Joel 2:23, 28, 29. (See our Tract No. 2, pp. 58, 59.) All who cheat themselves of this blessing, will seal their doom forever in the

Valley of Jezreel.

"Call his name Jezreel; for yet a little while, and I will avenge the blood of Jezreel upon the house of Jehu." Hos. 1:4.

As Jezreel typifies the prophets who have been killed, as well as those who today are being "killed" (rejected) by all who despise the gift of prophecy (1 Thess. 5:20), the valley of Jezreel, also, therefore is typical.

That is, as Jezreel represents the prophets, and as the "valley of Achor" (Hos. 2:15) stands for the destruction of those who are guilty of Achan's sin, then the "valley of Jezreel," the place where Jehu destroyed the rejecters of the prophets, (Hos. 1:5) must stand for the destruction of those who reject the Spirit of Prophecy today. Those who thus become disqualified and eliminated from being the Lord's servants in His final work, are to be succeeded by

The Laymen's Movement.

"Say ye [Jezreel] unto your brethren, Ammi; and to your sisters, Ruhamah. Plead with your mother, plead. . . ." Hos. 2:1, 2.

Here is brought to view a laymens' movement of both men and women who are to arise and proclaim the message of reformation to the church, their mother. They are to plead:

"Put away [your] whoredoms out of [your] sight, and [your] adulteries from between [your] breasts; lest [Father] strip [you] naked, and set [you] as in the day that [you were] born, and make [you] as a wilderness, and set [you] like a dry land, and slay [you] with thirst." Hos. 2:2, 3.

Through this personified prophecy, we see that the Lord is not now calling forth a "new" denomination, even though the ministry continues to take the membership rights from the adherents of this reformatory message. Consequently, for its successful delivery to the entire sisterhood of churches, our banding ourselves into a body of workers as a movement within a movement, has been *forced* upon us. In brief, we are to confine our message strictly to the old organization, as did the apostles with their message. For the first three and a half years after the resurrection, they were commissioned to put forth all their effort in behalf of their parent organization only, the last in the Old Testament period; likewise, the Davidians are commissioned to put forth an all-out effort in behalf of their parent, the Laodicean organization, the last in the New Testament period.

Let us confidently, therefore, work to the end of pressing together as an army with banners to proclaim the good tidings unto Zion. Then only can it be said of us: "How beautiful upon the mountains are the feet of him that bringeth good tidings, that publisheth peace; that bringeth good tidings of good, that publisheth salvation; that saith unto Zion, *Thy God reigneth!*" Isa. 52:7.

Brother, Sister, if you want a part in this never-so-glorious work, you dare not longer delay in lifting your voice to help warn "Mother" of what Father is about to do to her

Unlawful Children — "The Tares."

The church is charged with the terrible sin of whoredom,—intermingling with the world,—and of bringing forth "children of whoredoms" (Hos. 2:4), converts begotten not by "the Spirit of Truth" but by the spirit of the world.

These have not cut loose from the desires of the natural heart and from the promptings of the "carnal mind," the "lust of the eyes, and the pride of life"—all of which is "not of the Father, but is of the world." 1 John 2:16.

When these unlawful children are told of the straight testimony, which would compel them to give up the world and accept the whole truth, they quickly reveal themselves as not of the seed of God. Let dress and health reform and a thorough acceptance of the Spirit of Prophecy, without any mention of either worldly pleasures or sins of morality, be urged upon them, and thousands of so-called good Christians in unexceptionable standing in the church, will abandon their membership.

Let this test be applied, and the honest who may have some doubt about the results, will have it quickly and completely dispelled, once and forever. (*See Early Writings*, p. 270.) The church, well aware of this fact, and fearful that she may lose a selfish gain, tithes and offerings, if she fails to acquire a large membership, virtually says: "I will go after my lovers, that give me my bread and my water, my wool and my flax, mine oil and my drink. For she did not know," said the Lord, "that I gave her corn, and wine, and oil, and multiplied her silver and gold, which they prepared for Baal." Hos. 2:5, 8.

"Only when the church is composed of pure, unselfish members, can it fulfil God's purpose. Too much hasty work is done in adding names to the church roll. Serious defects are seen in the characters of some who join the church. Those who admit them say, We will first get them into the church, and then reform them. But this is a mistake. The very first work to be done is the work of reform. Pray with them, talk with them, but do not allow them to unite with God's people in church relationship until they give decided evidences that the Spirit of God is working upon their hearts."—*Review and Herald*, May 21, 1901, Vol. 78, No. 21.

"Thus peace and safety is the cry from men who will never again lift up their voice like a trumpet to show God's people their transgressions and the house of Jacob their sins. These dumb dogs, that would not bark, are the ones who feel the just vengeance of an offended God."—*Testimonies*, Vol. 5, p. 211.

"Yea, they are greedy dogs which can never have enough, and they are shepherds that cannot understand: they all look to their own way, every one for his gain, from his quarter" (Isa. 56:11)—the flock over which he has charge.

Because in their blind greed the shepherds have let the enemy mingle his "sheep" with the good flock, the Lord now, in a last rescue-effort, is commissioning

The Laity to Awake the Ministry.

In an effort to save our brethren from the imminent vengeance of God, the "great and dreadful day of the Lord" (Mal. 4:5), let every believer respond to the call of God, and unite his voice with the cry: "Awake, awake; put on thy strength, O Zion [by removing the accursed thing from among thee]; put on thy beautiful garments [Christ's righteousness], O Jerusalem, the holy city: for *henceforth* [after thou hast thus done] there shall no more come into thee the uncircumcised and the unclean." Isa. 52:1.

"And in that day shall the deaf hear the words of the book, and the eyes of the blind shall see out of obscurity, and out of darkness. The meek also shall increase their joy in the Lord, and the poor among men shall rejoice in the Holy One of Israel. For the terrible one is brought to naught, and the scorner is consumed, and all that watch for iniquity are cut off: that make a man an offender for a word, and lay a snare for him that reproveth in the gate, and turn aside the just for a thing of naught." Isa. 29:18-21.

Recline no longer, brother, sister: "Arise, shine; for thy light is come, and the glory of the Lord is risen upon thee." Isa. 60:1. "Behold, upon the mountains the feet of him that bringeth good tidings, that publisheth peace! O Judah, keep thy solemn feasts [the truth of the sanctuary], perform thy vows: for the wicked shall no more pass through thee; he is utterly cut off." Nah. 1:15.

"For Zion's sake," says the Lord, "will I not hold My peace, and for Jerusalem's sake I will not rest, until the righteousness thereof go forth as brightness, and the salvation thereof as a lamp that burneth. And the Gentiles shall see thy righteousness, and all kings thy glory: and thou shalt be called by a new name, which the mouth of the Lord shall name.

"Thou shalt also be a crown of glory in the hand of the Lord, and a royal diadem in the hand of thy God. Thou shalt no more be termed Forsaken; neither shall thy land any more be termed Desolate: but thou shalt be called Hephzibah, and thy land Beulah: for the Lord delighteth in thee, and thy land shall be married."

"I have set watchmen upon thy walls, O Jerusalem, which shall never hold their peace day nor night: ye that make mention of the Lord, keep not silence, and give Him no rest, till He establish, and till He make Jerusalem a praise *in the earth*." Isa. 62:1-4, 6, 7.

The message is now "disclosing to view" these wide awake watchmen.—*Testimonies*, Vol. 5, p. 80. And "he that is feeble among them at that day shall be as David; and the house of David shall be as God, as the angel of the Lord before them [before the great multitude of all nations]. And in that day will I make Jerusalem a burdensome stone for all people: all that burden themselves with it shall be cut in pieces, though all the people of the earth be gathered together against it." Zech. 12:8, 3.

And "in that day there shall be a fountain opened to the house of David and to the inhabitants of Jerusalem for sin and for uncleanness." "Many shall be purified, and made white, and tried; but the wicked shall do wickedly: and none of the wicked shall understand; but the wise shall understand." Zech. 13:1; Dan. 12:10.

"Then shall the offering of Judah and Jerusalem be pleasant unto the Lord, as in the days of old, and as in former years." Mal. 3:4.

"And I will rebuke the devourer for your sakes, and he shall not destroy the fruits of your ground; neither shall your vine cast her fruit before the time in the field, saith the Lord of hosts. And all nations shall call you blessed: for ye shall be a delightsome land, saith the Lord of hosts." Mal. 3:11, 12.

That your response to this heart-stirring call to service may be intelligently informed and whole-souled, you will, of course, be anxious to know

Where is God's Storehouse?

The Jewish church, in which reposed the truth up to the time of Christ, was ever to be "the storehouse," and the priests were ever to be its stewards. But when they rejected Christ, they forced God to transfer His "store-house" to the little handful who did accept the added message for that day. The unbelieving thereby un-wittingly forfeited their stewardship. Their followers who paid tithes to them from then on were diverting the Lord's money from His treasury to His enemies, to persecute His people. But those who were God's true people, followed "the Lamb whithersoever" He went, and "as many as were possessors of lands or houses sold them, and brought the prices of the things that were sold, and laid them down at the apostle's feet." Acts 4:34, 35.

For the benefit of those who may think that the tithe is used for the preaching of the gospel to the heathen only, we call their attention to the following instruc-tions: "These twelve Jesus sent forth, and command-ed them, saying, Go *not* into the *way* of the Gentiles, . . . but go rather to the lost sheep of the *house of Israel*." Matt. 10:5, 6. Nevertheless they received the tithes and offerings, and all that was laid at their feet before the message was extended to the Gentiles.

Later, God again transferred His storehouse, en-trusting its goods to the reformers who were stirred by the spirit of the down-trodden truth. Accordingly, His new and faithful stewards were appointed to care for the "candlestick," church, from then on. The third chapter of Malachi, as we have previously seen, is directly applicable to the purification of the church (see pages 33, 34). And the command, "bring ye all the tithes into the storehouse," being placed in this particular chapter of the Bible, shows beyond peradventure that God entrusts His "storehouse" to the messengers of the special truth for this time. And as this message is of as great importance to the church today as Christ's was to the Jewish church, we are equally bound by His command: "Let the children first be filled: for it is not meet to take the children's bread and to cast it unto the dogs" (heathen). Mark 7:27. Therefore, my brothers and sisters, take heed to the Word of God, and strictly comply with His command, lest with the workers of iniquity you fall under the "slaughter weapons" in horrible fulfilment of Ezekiel's vision.

Those who lived in the period of the old message, the judgment of the dead, were under obligation to support it, but now that we are entering into the period of the new message, the judgment of the living, we are duty-bound to support it. No longer is there either need or justification for our supporting the old message by itself, aloof from the new. No more so than there is in preaching Noah's prediction of the flood divorced from the future significance which derives from it.

". . . God does not want any man to think that no other message is to be heard but that which He may have given. We want the past message and the *fresh* message," says the Spirit of Prophecy.—*Review and Herald*, March 18, 1890.

Brother, Sister, unless you heed this solemn call, how shall you save your own souls, and how shall this message reach our brethren in the church, swell to a Loud Cry of the Third Angel's Message, and sound the judgment of the living? Will you take the bread from your own to feed it to the Gentiles, and thus have them both fall together in the "valley of Achor"?

The instructions in *The Shepherd's Rod*, Vol. 1, p. 251, "Pay your honest tithe and offering to your church, and feel that 'IT IS' your Father's house," came near the close of 1930, before the leading brethren, as a denomination, had rejected the sealing message. Clearly, then, *The Shepherd's Rod* has faithfully discharged its duty in refusing to accept any tithes or offerings until after the books were scattered throughout the denomination, and after the brethren began bitterly to oppose the message. Now, though, since the opposition is no longer passive, but intensely active, and the proclamation of the message supremely urgent, the only course open is apparent. It will take an army of workers, including the tithes and the offerings, to reach the people.

Consequently, as our leading brethren have inadvertently shown themselves unworthy stewards of God's "storehouse" for the time of the "Loud Cry of the Third Angel's Message," He has transferred the "candlestick" and is also calling for the tithes and offerings to be transferred into "His storehouse" of Present Truth.

When this great lay army has finished its work in the church, when it has escaped the slaying, then shall the Lord send them, as He says, "unto the nations, . . . that *have not heard* My fame, neither have seen My glory; and they shall declare My glory among the Gentiles. And they shall bring *all* your brethren for an offering unto the Lord out of *all* nations . . . in a *clean* vessel into the house of the Lord." Isa. 66:19, 20.

It follows, therefore, that unless the entire denomination be robbing Him, the Lord would not declare: "Ye have robbed Me, even this *whole nation*" (Mal. 3:9). But as most of the membership are paying tithes and offerings, the indictment proves that the funds are turned into a wrong treasury. And when could this be true save at the present time, when the denomination is fighting against God and His message with His Own money—the tithe? So it is that "even this whole nation" is robbing God. "Turn ye, turn ye from your evil ways; for why will ye die, O house of Israel?" Ezek. 33:11.

"Satan is constantly endeavoring to attract attention to man in the place of God.

He leads the people to look to bishops, to pastors, to professors of theology, as their guides, instead of searching the Scriptures to learn their duty for themselves. Then, by controlling the minds of these leaders, he can influence the multitudes according to his will.

"When Christ came to speak the words of life, the common people heard Him gladly; and many, even of the priests and rulers, believed on Him. *But the chief* of the priesthood and the *leading* men of the nation were determined to condemn and repudiate His teachings. Though they were baffled in all their efforts to find accusations against Him, though they could not but feel the influence of the divine power and wisdom attending His words, yet they encased themselves in prejudice; they rejected the clearest evidence of His Messiahship, lest they should be forced to become His disciples. These opponents of Jesus were men whom the people had been taught from infancy to reverence, to whose authority they had been accustomed implicitly to bow. 'How is it,' they asked, 'that our rulers and learned scribes do not believe on Jesus? Would not these pious men receive Him if He were the Christ?' It was the influence of such teachers that led the Jewish nation to reject their Redeemer. . . .

"Notwithstanding the Bible is full of warnings against false teachers, many are ready thus to commit the keeping of their souls to the clergy. There are today thousands of professors of religion who can give no other reason for points of faith which they hold than that they were so instructed by their religious leaders. They pass by the Saviour's teachings almost unnoticed, and place implicit confidence in the words of the ministers. But are ministers infallible? How can we trust our souls to their guidance unless we know from God's word that they are light-bearers? A lack of moral courage to step aside from the beaten track of the world, leads many to follow in the steps of learned men; and by their reluctance to investigate for themselves, they are becoming hopelessly fastened in the chains of error. They see that the truth for this time is plainly brought to view in the Bible, and they feel the power of the Holy Spirit attending its proclamation; yet they allow the opposition of the clergy to turn them from the light. Though reason and conscience are convinced, these deluded souls dare not think differently from the minister; and their individual judgment, their eternal interests, are sacrificed to the unbelief, the pride and prejudice, of another. . . .

"The truth and the glory of God are inseparable; it is impossible for us, with the Bible within our reach, to honor God by erroneous opinions. Many claim that it matters not what one believes, if his life is only right. But the life is moulded by the faith. If light and truth is within our reach, and we neglect to improve the privilege of hearing and seeing it we virtually reject it; we are choosing darkness rather than light."—*The Great Controversy*, pp. 595-597.

(Italic type ours)

SCRIPTURAL INDEX

"Blessed is he that readeth, and they that hear the words of this prophecy, and keep those things which are written therein: for the time is at hand." Rev. 1:3.